Pro Wrestling
Behind the Scenes

Michael Sandler

SCHOLASTIC INC.
New York   Toronto   London   Auckland   Sydney
Mexico City   New Delhi   Hong Kong

Cover photographs
© The Acci-Dent (top left and right)
© Duomo (bottom left and right)

Copyright ©2001 by Scholastic Inc.
All rights reserved. Published by Scholastic Inc.
Printed in the U.S.A.

ISBN 0-439-31284-1

SCHOLASTIC, READ 180, and associated logos and designs are trademarks and/or registered trademarks of Scholastic Inc.
LEXILE is a trademark of MetaMetrics, Inc.

3   4   5   6   7   8   9   10   40   11   12   13   14/0

Contents

1 Why Wrestling Rocks

"Rock! Rock! Rock!" The 20,000 fans chant louder and louder. An **arena** in Florida is packed with 20,000 fans screaming for their hero. His name is The Rock, a 6'5", 275-pound piece of granite. The Rock slams his enemy to the mat. Then he pins him. The crowd in the packed arena roars.

The wrestling hold that The Rock uses is not new. It is the same as one shown in a painting of wrestlers from ancient Egypt.

Professional wrestling has been around for about 50 years, but the sport of wrestling has been around for thousands of years—maybe longer. Historical records show that people tested their strength this way back in ancient times. Pictures of wrestlers have been found inside the tombs of Egyptian pharaohs. In Greek mythology, heroes Odysseus and Ajax wrestled each other. And at the first Olympics, held in Greece in 776 BC, wrestling was a main event. However, back then they didn't have outrageous costumes. They didn't even have team uniforms. They wrestled in the nude!

You can't tell who is fighting whom during this Battle Royal.

So why has wrestling been around for so long?

Some people consider the sport of wrestling pure competition. There is no equipment. There are no balls to catch, rackets to swing, or skates to lace. There are just two competitors, one-on-one, inside the ring.

Professional wrestling adds even more excitement. "Pro wrestling is all about good vs. evil," a fan said. "I like to root for the good guys to win. Pro wrestling is better than action movies!"

Fans can watch pro wrestling on cable TV nearly every day of the week. Professional wrestling programs are among the most popular shows on TV.

Why do you think professional wrestling is so popular?

2 Meet Ringmaster Vince McMahon

The most important man in pro wrestling doesn't even wrestle. Well, he almost never does. It's Vince McMahon, also known as the Ringmaster.

Today McMahon is well known as the owner of the World Wrestling Federation (WWF). But not everyone knows that McMahon singlehandedly changed the world of wrestling. To see how, you have to look back to an earlier time.

In the 1950s, 60s, and 70s, there were dozens of small wrestling leagues. Each league had its own wrestlers and its own local fans. Local television stations showed wrestling matches. But wrestling matches were never seen nationwide.

McMahon liked to think big, really big. He dreamed of starting a national league. In 1982, McMahon bought the WWF. At the time it was a small **regional** league. Then he began buying time on television stations across the U.S. Soon people in every state could see WWF matches. McMahon's wrestlers became known nationally. Large numbers of fans began to follow their adventures. The WWF wrestlers went from local heroes to superstars.

McMahon didn't just take professional wrestling to a larger audience. He added something more to it. He added big-style entertainment. McMahon created WrestleManias, Royal Rumbles, and SummerSlams. He added crazier costumes, heavy metal music, and lots of unsettled **grudges**. The wrestlers themselves became like soap opera characters. They got involved in long-running **feuds** and stories of revenge. Fans glued their eyes to the TV screen. They wanted to know what would happen next.

One wrestler in particular helped the WWF to grow. His name was Hulk Hogan. McMahon saw how audiences loved the Hulk

**Above: Ringmaster Vince McMahon brought
pro wrestling to a national audience.**

© Robert Beck/Timepix

Above: Hulk Hogan (left) battles Karl Malone.

in the movie *Rocky III*. So he brought Hogan into the WWF. From 1984 on, the giant 6'7" wrestler became a larger-than-life superstar. Hogan was a terrific wrestler and a natural showman. Hulkamania drew thousands of new fans to WWF matches.

Today, McMahon is still trying to pack more fans into the seats. He will do almost anything. No stunt is too strange. One night he took off his suit and stepped into the ring himself. He took on the wrestler Triple H for the WWF title. It looked like Triple H would pound McMahon into the mat. Then McMahon got a little help. Stone Cold Steve Austin jumped into the ring. Austin held Triple H down while McMahon pinned him. For a brief moment, McMahon was champion of his own league!

Wrestler Owen Hart paid the ultimate price for one of these dramatic stunts. In 1999, at a WWF match in Kansas City, Hart was being lowered into the ring from high up in the arena. Suddenly the harness that held him accidentally opened. Hart plunged to his death in front of the audience. Vince McMahon got some of the blame.

Some people feel that professional wrestling is no longer a sport. They say it's become like a circus, thanks to Vince McMahon.

How did Vince McMahon change the world of pro wrestling?

3 Behind the Scenes

Think being a pro wrestler is easy? Think again. Each time two 250-pounders **collide**, anything can happen. Take a look at WWF star Mick Foley. Foley has been called "the world's most injured man." During his career, he's had six concussions, received 325 stitches, and broken his ribs five times. As Foley knows, a wrestling match can be a dangerous event.

The average pro wrestler may fight 250 matches a year. To survive all this punishment, wrestlers need power, flexibility, and timing. How do they build their bodies to hold up to these demands? How do they master the holds and throws they need to survive? The answer is training, and plenty of it.

Top wrestlers never stop training. There is a lot to learn and a lot to master. Here are some of the things wrestlers work on.

Strength Pro wrestlers spend plenty of time working with weights. They like to use full body lifts. Some full body lifts include the clean-and-jerk and the hang-clean. These lifts build overall muscle strength and coordination.

Conditioning Wrestlers need to develop stamina, or staying power, to keep going round after round. So they are always working on their conditioning. That may mean jogging, hitting the Stairmaster, or spending hours on the exercise bike. Many wrestlers run four to five miles each day.

Flexibility It may be hard to believe, but those hard bodies are some of the most flexible ones around. Wrestlers spend hours stretching. They know that flexibility is important in the ring. It's a key to avoiding injury.

Bret Hart maintains a strict exercise program to keep in shape.

Technique You can never have too much technique. That's what the pros say. It's not just about throwing and pinning other wrestlers. Technique also means knowing what to do when you are the one being pinned, dropped, slammed, or thrown. Wrestlers spend hours each day mastering moves like the sit-and-roll, the pile driver, and the leg drop.

Photo: AP Photo/Gail Burton

At a school for professional wrestling, a teacher demonstrates the proper way to do a headlock.

Some wrestlers have come up with unusual practice routines. In 1999, megastar Goldberg was starring in his first movie. He wanted to keep his 285-pound body in shape. So in between scenes, he did some special exercises. He picked up members of the film crew and lifted them over his head.

Why is it important for wrestlers to stay in shape?

4 Women Warriors

Pro wrestling isn't just a man's game. Throughout the years, there have been plenty of women warriors.

The most famous one may be the Fabulous Moolah. She's the only female wrestler in the WWF's Hall of Fame. Moolah held the women's title for 28 straight years. Her reign as queen of pro wrestling came to an end in 1984. That year, she was finally defeated by Wendi "150 pounds of steel" Richter.

Many of today's women wrestlers began their careers as bodyguards and managers. They worked for some of the biggest stars in pro wrestling. Stalking the aisles outside the ring, these tough women helped protect the

Photo: © Steve Sutton/Duomo

Sable and Tori battle it out in the ring.

stars from overeager fans. Many women began to ask why men should have the fun and fame. Soon they jumped into the ring themselves.

Chyna, for example, began her career as Triple H's bodyguard. Now the 5'10", 200-pounder is a body slam specialist. She can bench press 365 pounds. She'll wrestle men or women. Either way, she almost always wins.

Madusa Micelli is also among the best. The 5'9", 150-pound powerhouse went to Japan to perfect her skills. When she returned to the U.S., she became a star. In the early 1990s, Madusa retired from wrestling. She decided to sharpen her skills as a world-class kickboxer instead.

Sable is the femme-fatale of female wrestling. Once she was a fashion model. Then she decided that the ring was the place to be. Soon she slammed her way to the top of the pack as WWF women's champion. No one could stand up to Sable's signature move, the Sablebomb.

Sable's only problem is her own popularity. She can't walk down the street without fans screaming her name. "Whether it's the local McDonalds or the doctor's office, I'm recognized," says Sable. "But I don't mind it. If it weren't for the fans, where would I be?"

The women aren't just sticking to the men's leagues. There's also a new group called WOW. WOW stands for Women of Wrestling. With stars such as Bambi, Hammerin' Heather Steele, and GI Joan, WOW wants to move in on the older leagues. These women are ready to grab the spotlight.

Why do you think women wrestlers want their own league?

5 A Day in the Life

Ever wonder what it's like to be a pro wrestling megastar like Bill Goldberg? Well, read on to find out.

Weighing almost 300 pounds, William Scott Goldberg is the size of a pro football lineman. It's not surprising. Goldberg used to play defense in the National Football League (NFL). Injuries ended his football career.

That's when Goldberg switched to pro wrestling. Quickly he excelled, winning his first 170 fights in a row. Almost right away, he became a star.

Wrestling came easily to Goldberg. Stardom is another story.

"You wouldn't believe my schedule," says Goldberg. "It's overwhelming."

Goldberg's day usually starts with a drive to the airport. In a normal week, Goldberg might travel to five or six different towns. Sometimes it's hard for him to remember where the next match takes place. So he checks his airplane ticket to find out.

Once he arrives, Goldberg heads to a local TV station. He needs to do promotions for the evening's big event.

Right: **Goldberg pins his opponent.**

Below: **Goldberg congratulates a young winner at the Arnold Physical Fitness Expo.**

Photo The Acci-Dent

Then it's over to a nearby hospital. Goldberg often donates his free time to cheer up sick kids. He likes to use his stardom to help others. Sometimes he helps the Make-a-Wish Foundation. This group raises money to grant the wishes of dying children.

Now it's time for lunch. He stops at his hotel and orders hot dogs, fries, and pizza. Eating this way would make most people fat. But wrestlers

need lots of calories. They burn off plenty in the ring.

Arriving at the arena, Goldberg prepares in his dressing room. Unlike many wrestlers, he doesn't go for crazy costumes. Goldberg doesn't have any **gimmicks**. He likes to keep it simple. He wears gloves, wrestling trunks, and his trademark goatee beard.

No one has to tell Goldberg when it's time to walk down to the ring. He can hear the crowd chanting: Gold-berg! Gold-berg! Gold-berg! The roar of the fans is incredibly loud.

Tonight Goldberg takes on Rick Steiner. The two warriors battle for nearly 30 minutes. Finally Goldberg uses a jackhammer move to win the match.

But Goldberg still isn't done for the day. Tonight, he has to make another trip to the hospital. This time, he's getting some stitches for a cut he got in the ring.

At last he heads back to the hotel. There's still work to be done. First he checks his messages. He gets many offers to go on television shows and requests for public appearances. Then, he hops into bed.

But Goldberg doesn't nod off yet. He has a little bedtime reading to do. This is when he reads through some movie scripts that people in Hollywood have sent him. All the studios, it seems, want Goldberg in their film.

At last it's off to sleep. He knows that once the alarm clock rings, the fast pace starts all over. So with all the money and fame that stardom brings, what Goldberg would really like is a relaxing day at home. Unfortunately, he only gets back to his home in Dawsonville, Georgia, for a few days every month.

Would you want to be a professional wrestler? Why or why not?

# Is It Fake?

Over the years pro wrestling has had its **critics**. Again and again, they have brought up the same issue. Wrestling is not a sport, they charge. The matches are fake.

Many wrestling fans deny it. They believe wrestling is a sport.

Who is right? The critics or the fans?

Once and for all, we're going to settle the question. We're going to reveal the secret truth about wrestling. We're going to answer the question. Is wrestling fake? Here's the answer: yes! and no!

Confused? Let's explain.

Wrestling matches are scripted. The wrestlers are like actors who play their roles.

The Rock battles Stone Cold Steve Austin.

Before a match takes place, both wrestlers know who's going to win. They know who's going to lose. Often they rehearse the exact moves.

The truth came out in New Jersey. The wrestling leagues wanted to save a little money. If a sports event is televised in New Jersey, its organizers have to pay a special tax. The wrestling leagues didn't want to pay this tax. So they told the truth. Wrestling is entertainment, not a sport. Unlike a real sporting event, a wrestling match is planned.

But even if the winners are chosen in advance, the action is real. It takes real skill and real strength to perform the **maneuvers** that fans love to see. And even with practice, a wrestler can get injured—for real.

One former wrestling official, Carl DeMarco, says, "The moves are real. When a guy gets slammed, he's really getting slammed!"

Indeed the punishment that wrestlers take is not fake. They get real bruises and real sprains. And yes, it really hurts to get pounded into a turnbuckle by a 350-pound opponent.

Wrestlers may use fake blood once in awhile, but just as often, they don't need to. There's no doubt about it, wrestling is not for the weak!

Another thing that is real about pro wrestling is that only the best wrestlers get to become champions. If a lousy wrestler started winning title belts, the fans wouldn't accept it. They could tell right away that the wrestler wasn't any good.

The fans have the last word. To them, it just doesn't seem to matter. "Fake or not," says one long-time fan, "wrestling sure is fun."

Do you care if pro wrestling is real? Why or why not?

7 The Hitman's Battle

Pro wrestling mixes red-hot entertainment and cold, hard business. Don't think so? Check out what happened to Bret "The Hitman" Hart and see the cold side of pro wrestling for yourself.

Hart lived and breathed wrestling from an early age. His seven brothers all became pro wrestlers. His father, Stu, was a wrestling pioneer. He ran an organization called Stampede Wrestling.

When Hart was a child, he would find Stampede wrestlers sitting around the kitchen table. Sometimes they'd be training in the basement. In time, Hart became a wrestler himself. He learned the tricks of the trade from two Japanese wrestlers in the Stampede. They taught him 50 ways to throw a wrestler to the mat.

In 1984, Hart joined the WWF. He called himself "The Hitman." Then he joined wrestler Jimmy Neidhart. The two formed the "Hart Foundation" tag team. They were the roughest, toughest duo on the WWF circuit. They wore flashy costumes. Their famous slogan was "The best there is. The best there was. The best there ever will be."

Then in 1991 Hart went solo. He won his first title by crushing Curt "Mr. Perfect" Hennig. He drew thousands of fans and wrestled 250 days a year.

As five-time WWF champion, the 6-foot, 235-pound Hart became wrestling's brightest star. Soon the other big wrestling group, the WCW (World Champion Wrestling), tried to steal him away. The WCW offered Hart $9 million. If he took their offer, he'd be the world's second highest-paid wrestler. Only Hulk Hogan earned more.

But Hart didn't want to leave the WWF. He had spent more than ten years in that league.

**Bret "The Hitman" Hart in his controversial match against
Shawn Michaels.**

"I had a loyalty to my fans," he explained. Then WWF owner Vince McMahon made Hart an offer. According to Hart, McMahon assured him he would be with the WWF for life.

Hart showed his loyalty. He stayed in the WWF. Then Hart got some stunning news. He wasn't going to be a WWF good guy anymore. He would be a villain. His character would get a pro-Canada, anti-U.S. twist. McMahon thought fans would pack the arenas to root for Hart to lose.

Hart didn't mind being a villain. But he didn't like trashing the U.S. He felt that would be the same as trashing his own fans. He would lose the popularity he had worked so hard for.

Then McMahon dropped the bomb. He told Hart to forget about that "lifetime" contract. Hart had enough. He decided that he would join the WCW. But first he had to finish his WWF career.

His last big match was with his enemy Shawn Michaels. Before it began, Hart and McMahon discussed how the match would end.

Hart would have to lose his title. McMahon

didn't want Hart leaving while holding the WWF belt.

They agreed on a plan. During the match, Shawn Michaels would trap Hart in a "sharpshooter" hold. Hart would get out of it. There would be a brawl. It would end in a disqualification. In the WWF, this was an honorable defeat. Hart wouldn't really lose. But he would give up the belt as McMahon demanded.

But that's not how it happened. During the match, Michaels put Hart into a hold called the "sharpshooter." Suddenly the referee rang the bell. The fight was over. Hart had lost. It seemed like McMahon tricked Hart into leaving as a loser.

How do you feel about what happened to Bret Hart?

8 The Ruling Body

Do you think that wrestlers are just "dumb jocks"? Think again! Plenty of wrestlers have shown their smarts by achieving success outside the ring. Some, such as Rowdy Roddy Piper and Hulk Hogan, have starred in movies and on television. The most impressive story, however, belongs to Jesse "The Body" Ventura.

For 11 years Jesse Ventura was a top WWF bad guy. At 6'4" he was known for dark sunglasses, pink tights, and a powerful body. In fact, this body earned him his nickname. Jesse was very proud of it. As he said at the time, "I'm the most beautiful man in wrestling today, without a doubt."

After years in the ring, The Body retired to

his hometown of Brooklyn Park, Minnesota. In 1990 Ventura began to think that his town needed improving. He wanted to change things. So he decided to run for mayor. To many people's surprise, Ventura won the election. He spent four years as mayor. During that time, he focused on fighting crime.

When his term as mayor ended, Ventura returned to the wrestling world. He worked as a WCW **commentator**. He spent a few more years acting in movies and hosting radio shows. But then he was struck once more by the political itch. He decided to run for governor.

At first people didn't take Ventura seriously. How could a man who used to bodyslam opponents while wearing pink tights become governor? Comedians around the country made jokes about the wrestler.

Ventura, however, wasn't running for laughs. He impressed the people of Minnesota with his positions on the issues. One thing he felt strongly about was education. Schools, said Ventura, were important. He promised that if he were elected, he would make them better for Minnesota's kids.

Photo: AP Photo/Dawn Villella

Governor Jesse Ventura promises to bring law and order back to wrestling as a guest referee.

Ventura faced an uphill battle. He wasn't a Democrat, and he wasn't a Republican. He ran as a member of the Reform party. To get people to take him seriously, he campaigned all over the state. When election day came, no one was laughing anymore. Ventura had won the race.

The Body became governor of Minnesota. Once in office, Ventura began his important work. Right away he set out to tackle the big issues—jobs, education, and crime.

What's next for Ventura? Nobody knows for sure. Some people think that he may run for President of the United States! Just imagine what that would do for the popularity of professional wrestling. It could replace baseball as the national pastime.

Why did people take Jesse Ventura seriously when he ran for office?

Glossary

arena a large area that is used for sports or entertainment

collide to crash together forcefully, often at high speed

commentator a person who describes the action and comments during an event

critics people who point out what's wrong with something

feuds bitter quarrels between people that last for a long time

gimmicks clever costumes, tricks, or ideas used to get people's attention

grudges feelings of anger and resentment toward someone who has hurt or insulted you in the past

maneuvers difficult movements that need planning and skill

regional belonging to a certain area or district